SAIGON

HO CHI MINH CITY

Klaus H. Carl

Publishing Director: Jean-Paul Manzo

Text: Klaus H.Carl

Translation from German: Jane Ennis

Design and layout: Matthieu Carré

Photograph credits: © Klaus H.Carl

© Parkstone Press Ltd, New-York, USA, 2003
Printed and bound in Slovakia.
ISBN 1 85995 719 6

SAIGON
HO CHI MINH CITY
Klaus H. Carl

CONTENTS

A brook cut from its source drains away and dries up.
A tree deprived of its roots withers away.
A revolutionary without morals will never achieve his goals.
(Ho Chi Minh)

A Permanent Process of Change

Saigon — a name that evokes memories of the colonial period, tragedies such as the Indochina and Vietnam wars, the division of the country into North and South Vietnam, or the fleeing boat people and their wretched plight.

It is the world-famous name of a town that was once known as "The Pearl of the Orient" or "The Paris of the East", which is now striving unceasingly to regain its former reputation. Saigon is not Ho Chi Minh City, but merely one of many districts in a central administrative region of the same name, containing about six million inhabitants, and covering an area of at least 2,000 square km. In the immediate catchment area there are at least 18 million inhabitants. Cholon, formerly Chinatown and now amalgamated with Saigon, belongs to this administrative region, as does the agricultural sector Cu Chi (approximately 50 km west of Saigon) and Gia Dinh. Especially in South Vietnam, people only use the name Saigon, even if the whole conurbation of Ho Chi Minh City is meant.

In order to understand this, a brief outline of recent Vietnamese history is necessary. It had originally been intended to allow the two states of North and South Vietnam to continue to exist independently for five years after the armistice of

1. Balloons for the New Year
2. Greeting cards
3. A Young Vietnamese woman
   with her child

1973. However, the refugee problem and economic difficulties in a region that had become almost ungovernable, pushed the government in Hanoi into unification earlier than intended, and also forced it to call elections in 1976. In July 1976 the country was proclaimed The Socialist Republic of Vietnam. Saigon, already recognised as the undisputed economic centre of Vietnam, became the core of the city-state "*Than Pho Ho Chi Minh*".

Saigon is a relatively young city. Originally known as *Gia Dinh*, it was founded in 1764 by the Vietnamese on the site of fishing villages previously occupied by the Khmer – whom the Vietnamese expelled – at Song Sai Gon, in a lowland plain on the northern side of the Mekong Delta, approximately 50 km from the coast. It owes its present-day structure to the French, who conquered the city on 1859, meeting hardly any resistance from the Vietnamese. To their surprise the French were also offered the surrounding provinces by Emperor *Tu Duc* – an offer that a colonial power simply could not refuse – and they immediately set

4. Buildings overlooking
Minh Square

out to plan and develop the city on the Parisian model, with wide avenues and boulevards. The typical buildings – post office, opera house, town hall and of course a cathedral dedicated to "Notre Dame" – were built during this period.

At first Saigon was merely the capital of the colony of Cochin China, then it became the seat of the colonial administration of Indochina, and in 1954, when the Treaty of Geneva confirmed the end of French colonial rule in Indochina, Saigon was proclaimed the capital of the Republic of South Vietnam.

The city changed a second time under American influence, during the period of the Vietnam War. The Vietnamese, who fought so desperately, call it "The American War". The American forces needed bars, amusement arcades, supermarkets and massage parlours for their off-duty personnel, and people to work in all these establishments. In order to partake of the blessings of the dollar as shoe cleaners, taxi-drivers or maids, people were torn from their traditional family structures and poured into this supposed paradise from the surrounding

5. The view from Le Duan Street

— 9 —

countryside until it was full to bursting, living in hastily erected slums on the outskirts of the city. In fact, there were never more beggars, drug addicts or prostitutes than at this time, during which much more than half the population were dependent for their livelihood on the Americans, who had built an entire garrison town. The famous Rue Catinat of the "Paris of the Orient", leading directly from the river to the cathedral, degenerated into "The Brothel of Vietnam". *Tu Do* (meaning freedom), now known as *Dong Khoi*, became the nightclub quarter of Saigon, with its hundreds of bars and hotels where rooms could be rented by the hour. The town became the undisputed sleaze capital of the world. Hotel bars were rendezvous points for diplomats and journalists, and thus became rumour mills in which gossip became opinion and real or imagined facts became dogmas.

6. Glass facade
7. Glass facade

This did not change after until the American withdrawal and the takeover by North Vietnam in April 1975. The number of inhabitants in Saigon had almost doubled and an attempt was made to solve the problem of overpopulation by compulsory resettlement. Hundreds of thousands of Saigonese were transferred to hastily established, barely functioning "New Economic Zones". These failed, however, due not only to the fact that there was no financial assistance for the people who had been moved into these areas, but because the Vietnamese have extended families which are very much rooted in their native land and practice ancestor worship.

Many of the remaining inhabitants of Saigon also lost their jobs, or could not find jobs for which their qualifications were appropriate. Furthermore, it was a region orientated almost entirely towards agriculture, and basic industries either did not exist, or could not function because spare parts were unavailable. Saigon's situation deteriorated further after 1978, when the campaign against the black market – mainly run by the Chinese with goods from Thailand – intensified. Many self-employed professionals, especially doctors and pharmacists, had already left the town and fled abroad, taking their assets with them. Now the forced expropriation of the Chinese traders' goods drove them also to take flight

8. The Saigon River
9. Dwellings along the Thi Nighe canal in the Botanical Gardens district

10. Dwellings along the
Saigon River

across the sea. They too took all their moveable assets with them. The plight of these "*boat people*" often attracted the attention of the media, especially the tabloid press.

The third phase of change began at the end of the 1980s and the beginning of the 1990s, as gangs of building workers tackled the urgent needs of restoration and modernisation in their city. A few years earlier, a bicycle had represented the highest aim in life. Today more than a million motorcycles inch their way through the crowded streets.

The inhabitants of Saigon have new dreams: of cars, or homes in the suburbs, since the rents in the inner city are now comparable with those in Singapore and other large cities of this region. This is of course especially true of young people – approximately half of the inhabitants of Saigon were born after 1975 – who are drawn to the city from the rest of Vietnam. But many Vietnamese who fled into exile to escape the Communists are now returning, and since the mid-1990s, foreign investment capital has created a building boom (although there are also some investment failures). Now the clouds are reflected in the characterless, boring, glass exteriors of the skyscrapers just the same as in the skyscrapers of capital cities the world over. Saigon is the headquarters of the Chief Buddhist of Vietnam, as well as of a Catholic Archbishop. The city has two universities and an Institute of Agriculture, as well as many research institutes and an Academy of Art.

11. Dwellings along the
Saigon River

Geography

Vietnam is situated on the edge of South-East Asia and covers a total area of approximately 330,000 square km. Nestling against the eastern edge of the mainland, it resembles an elongated "S". The "S" begins in the North at the Gulf of Tonkin, where it shares a border with Southern China. It continues southward through the western mountains, along the common border with Laos and Cambodia for a distance of 1,600 km, extending southeast as far as the Gulf of Thailand (previously the Gulf of Siam). The South China Sea constitutes its eastern border. The Vietnamese coast is about 3,200 km. in length, and its splendid sandy beaches have up till now been spared the incursions of tourism. Offshore there are thousands of islands and islets, mainly uninhabited. The largest is *Phu Quoc*, about 570 square km, off the southwest coast, close to Laos. The most notorious is the prison island *Con Dao*, on the other side of the southern tip of Vietnam. Not only was this the place of detention for political prisoners during the colonial period, but several members of the North Vietnamese government later spent years of imprisonment here. Now all the islands, and the detention centres, can be visited. During the Vietnam War, high-yielding deposits of oil were discovered off the southern coast. Because of the lack of refineries, most of it had to be exported. Since then, oil and natural gas have made substantial contributions to the economic growth of Vietnam.

The broadest expanse of Vietnam's landmass — about 600 km from east to west — is in the north. The narrowest is the central region — only a stone's throw across 50 km or so. Near the borders with neighbouring countries there are densely forested, sparsely populated mountain ranges, which hardly ever reach a height of more than 2,000 m. (The highest mountain, at least 3,140 m high, is in the northwest.) In the jungle areas here are still to be found animals that can be found nowhere else. At the beginning of the 1990s there was great excitement in the media at reports of a previously unknown species of antelope, and, a few years later, of the *Muntjac* deer.

The sources of about 2,500 rivers are located in the mountain peaks. The Mekong, which rises in Tibet, is about 4,500 km long, which makes it one of the

12. Bronze plaque from the Tran Hung Dao monument illustrating Vietnamese men preparing for war

16. Street children

Kiang into what is now Vietnam. Early written records point to the year 207 BC when a Chinese general rebelled against the Emperor and founded the country *Nam Viet* ("Land of the non-Chinese"), of which he styled himself king. The country extended into southern China, as can clearly be seen from the location of its capital close to *Guangzhou* (Canton). About 100 years later, in 111 BC, the Chinese captured the Red River Delta and made it into a colony which they named Giao Chi ("Land of the bare-footed people"). After the legendary Hung Dynasty, which is presumed to have ruled from about 1480 to 248 BC (although there are no records to confirm this), the Chinese Han Dynasty came to power and re-incorporated the area into their southern region. Despite repeated rebellions by the Vietnamese, they were unable to put an end to the Chinese oppression that ensued. The most important were: the rebellion led by the Trung sisters between 40-43 AD (who are said to have thrown themselves into the Red River to avoid capture), a rebellion led by Trieu Au around 248 AD (a woman who is always depicted with huge breasts), and later that of the Black Emperor Mai Thuc Loan around 722 AD. Only in 939 AD did Ngo Quyen succeed in defeating the Chinese in a battle near Haiphong and driving them out.

It was at about this time that the Vietnamese, whose own name for themselves was "*kinh*", began to move further south from the over-populated Red River Delta. After many years of conflict, they began to drive out the Cham from their

kingdom of Champa. The Cham were Hindus who had long before migrated from Indonesia. Between the sixth and the tenth centuries they controlled a large part of the spice trade, and were widely feared as pirates. Champa existed roughly from the seventh century to the seventeenth and was located in the central region of what is now Vietnam. These were not brief battles or confrontations – on the contrary, the conflict lasted for about 700 years, although there were brief periods of co-operation, when for instance it was necessary to oppose the Mongols of Kublai Khan and bar their access to the sea.

The art of the Cham, which has still not been exhaustively researched, developed independently. A script similar to South Indian Sanskrit is found on their stelae. Their kings fulfilled the office of god-kings, unifying all power in themselves, and their symbol was the lingam, a phallic symbol. The last king of the Cham fled to the mountains of neighbouring Cambodia.

The Viet also drove out the numerically inferior Khmer from their territory in the Mekong Delta; the Khmer had dominated large areas of South-East Asia between the tenth and the fourteenth centuries. It is only thanks to the magnificent temple complex at Angkor that more information is now available about Khmer art. Their social structure, with its divine kings and the court nobility, showed very close parallels with the royal court of the Cham. The Khmer retained some fishing villages at the confluence of the Ben-Nghe and Son Sai Gon rivers. According to legend, this river was inhabited by crocodiles who sounded more like buffaloes, and this was how the settlement came by its name of *Ben-Nghe* – "buffalo jetty", which it still bore when the Viet reached this area at the end of the last quarter of the 17th century. The town was then called *Ben Thanh* (there is a market of that name in Saigon to this day). Its current name was bestowed some time between 1728 and 1785 by Le Yui Don of the restored Le dynasty.

The Colonial Period

In the mid-16th century the Portuguese, who had been granted dominion over "the eastern half of the world" by Pope Alexander VI [1], (the "western half of the world" belonged to Spain, thanks to the Treaty of Tordesillas of 1494), founded their first fortified settlement, equipped with canons, on the site of present-day Hoi An (south of Da Nang). This was not only a trading base, but also a base for an unwelcome attempt to introduce Christian missionaries into Vietnam, a country in which Confucianism was firmly rooted. The Portuguese, however, were not the only colonists, since the British, the French and the Dutch also had a presence in Vietnam. The Dutch were already established in Indonesia, and the French were concerned – not without cause – that the British might overtake them in the scramble for power in South East Asia, as the latter had already consolidated their power bases in India and Singapore. The French, however, had one advantage over their competitors: the French Jesuit Alexandre de Rhodes had transcribed the Vietnamese language into Latin characters. Furthermore, Pigneau de Béhaine, the Bishop of Adran, was in the confidence of Prince Nguyen Anh, whom he had rescued from rebels when he was 16 years old.

17. Glass facade

18. Doorway

The Twentieth Century

The Communist Party of Vietnam (*Viet Nam Cong San Dang*) was founded in 1930 by Ai Quoc, a revolutionary who went under many pseudonyms, finally adopting the name *Ho Chi Minh*[4]. Today he is still referred to respectfully as *Bac Ho* (Uncle Ho). In 1940, when he returned from a decade of exile in Asia and Europe, he founded the "league for an independent Vietnam", the *Viet Minh*, and organised resistance as its leader.

Japan, one of the Axis powers in the Second World War, had already invaded Vietnam in 1941. They had driven out the French and, in order to simplify matters, had for a short time installed as Emperor Bao Dai, who had already served the French in this capacity. But in August 1945 Japan surrendered after Hiroshima and Nagasaki, and Bao Dai abdicated. Ho Chi Minh led the August Revolution, as a result of which he proclaimed the independence of the Democratic Republic of Vietnam (DRV) on 2 September 1945. The DRV was recognised as a Free State by the French, on condition that Hanoi accepted ultimate French sovereignty.

24. Young woman on a scooter

25. Scene illustrating the typically dense street traffic

Following pages:

26. Rickshaw

The peace that ensued was deceptive; already in 1946 there had been an incident between the French and the Vietnamese in the Gulf of Tonkin that led to war between France and Vietnam (1946-1954). After fierce fighting, the war finally ended on 7 May 1954 with the decisive battle of Dien Bien Phu when the Vietnamese surrendered the small jungle fortress in North Vietnam, on the border with Laos, which had hitherto been considered impregnable. The DRV signed an armistice agreement at the Geneva Conference on 20 July 1954, supported by Stalin's successors[5] in the Soviet Union, and by Mao's China[6]. This treaty designated a demarcation line at the 17th Parallel, and contained an agreement that free and universal elections were to be held within two years. The country was partitioned in a fashion similar to the division of Germany and Korea at this period. President and Chief Minister Ho Chi Minh ruled in the Communist North, while in the South, which had been re-named The Republic of South Vietnam, the Diem regime supported by the USA had taken power. Since the free elections promised in the armistice agreement did not take place, despite repeated demands by the North Vietnamese government, mass migration occurred. Troops from Hanoi moved north with their dependents, while Catholic Vietnamese moved from the Democratic Republic of Vietnam to the Catholic Diem regime in the South. Population displacement was a problem that led to frequent attempted coups against Diem who, however, was still supported by the Americans. In 1962 the USA established an 8,000 strong commando unit in Saigon and over the next four years this increased in size to about 400,000. The intention was to keep South Vietnam on the side of the West. Diem was not deposed until the end of 1963. He and his brother, accompanied by a military escort, sought refuge in the Catholic Church of Cha Dam in Cholon, but during the journey to the centre of Saigon both men were assassinated by their escort. Diem's government was replaced by various emergency cabinets. In August 1964 there was another incident in the fateful Gulf of Tonkin, this time between North Vietnamese and American warships, which increased the latent tensions between the USA and North Vietnam.

The official date for the beginning of this terrible war, which was conducted with extreme brutality, was 8 March 1965 when American troops landed in Da Nang. All in all, 40,000 tonnes of bombs were dropped — not to mention the tonnes of herbicides that were sprayed. Terrible devastation was caused, not only by the herbicides. The Viet Cong captured the demilitarised zone between North and South Vietnam in 1967, and began the Tet Offensive on 1 January 1968. The war appeared to be at an end with the signing of an armistice agreement on 27 January 1973. In spite of the appointment of an International Control Commission, however, conflicts continued to flare up. In the course of these, the North Vietnamese made considerable territorial gains south of the 17th Parallel. The decisive breakthrough did not come until 1975 and the last Americans left the country on 30 April 1975, just hours before North Vietnamese troops occupied the Presidential Palace in Saigon and hoisted the North Vietnamese flag. In July 1976 Saigon was given a new name - *Ho Chi Minh City*.

This war also left its mark on the West, both in the USA and in Europe. It began with peaceful demonstrations, then as the war continued the demonstrations became more violent, leading to street fighting and clashes, and sometimes to situations resembling civil war. It was mainly students and young people who were involved in these protests; they did not see why democracy had to be defended in Vietnam, of all places. They had no time for the domino-theory of their governments, who had long since lost all credibility in their eyes, and they articulated their protests against this war and the hated "Establishment".

The "Generation of '68" grew out of this protest movement, which in the medium and long term did in fact lead to a change in the concept of what "democracy" means, and to a change of outlook in many other areas.

The country was indeed now re-unified, but it had been bled dry during the colonial period and the brutal wars. Vietnam was now one of the poorest countries in the world. The American withdrawal had led to the closure of many processing plants and thus to increased unemployment, rapidly growing inflation and black market activity. In order to combat this, private businesses in South Vietnam were nationalised in March 1978. The result was that thousands of war profiteers, mainly Chinese living in Vietnam, tried to flee abroad with their families, often taking with them vast fortunes. It is impossible even to guess how many of these refugees – known as "boat people" – managed to reach their goals, and how many fell into the hand of pirates or thieves and may even have been killed.

In 1979 Vietnamese troops marched into Cambodia and liberated it from the murderous Khmer Rouge troops of the grisly Pol Pot regime, which was supported by China. They did not withdraw until the autumn of 1989. In the same

28. Cyclists protect themselves from dust

year re-privatisation took place and Vietnam gradually regained its position as the world's third largest rice-exporter. In 1990 there was a breakthrough in the West's relationship with Vietnam when the first talks between Vietnam and the USA took place. In the same year, Japan, Taiwan and South Korea became Vietnam's most important trading partners. In 1993 Vietnam received financial assistance from the IMF and the World Bank for the first time, and President Clinton lifted the embargo against Vietnam a year later. Finally, normal diplomatic relations between the USA and Vietnam were introduced in July 1995.

Population

The population has grown rapidly. At the end of the 19th century Vietnam had about ten million inhabitants. By 1976 the population had grown to 50 million, and by 1990 had reached about 65 million. Today the population is reckoned to be about 80 million, with an average age of under thirty. Of these 80 million, about five million live in the conurbation of Ho Chi Minh City – two million in

29. Night parade to celebrate the New Year

Following pages:
30. Night parade to celebrate the New Year

Saigon alone — and about 3.5 million in the city state of Hanoi, although there are only about one and a half million in the capital Hanoi itself. The increase is clearly demonstrated by population density: in 1945 there were 21 inhabitants per square km, in 1999 this had increased to 237. (In comparison, there are 27 inhabitants per square km in the USA, 22 in Laos, 119 in neighbouring Thailand, and 229 in Germany[7]) Today Vietnam is one of the 20 most densely populated countries in the world, although in 1990 it was ranked 75th. An increase of 1.5% per annum means that every year there are about 1.2 million more mouths to feed. As life expectancy is increasing at the same rate - it was 65 years in 1995, this places the population of Vietnam at 119th in the world ranking. Such an annual increase implies huge problems for a largely rural population— about 80% of Vietnamese still live in rural areas — because Vietnam's cultivable land only covers an expanse of about 90,000 square km.

There are 54 ethnic groups, of which the largest is the Viet, who constitute approximately 90% of the entire population. The Viet are presumed to have originally migrated from the Tibet-Mongolia region, and to have intermarried with the inhabitants of the southern region of China, and also with ethnic groups migrating from Eastern Indonesia. Based on the above-mentioned figures for the total population, there are about eight million members of various ethnic minorities. The groups usually consist of about 700,000 to a million members, but there are also some groups of between 100 to 500 members who live in inaccessible areas of the highlands of South-East Asia, often straddling national frontiers. These small groups are predominantly members of mountain tribes; they breed cattle or practice dry cultivation of rice. Other minorities include roughly equal numbers of Khmer and Chinese, and a small number of Cham.

31. Young Vietnamese girls during the New Years celebration in the Botanical Gardens district
32. Selling balloons

Religions

Animism, the archetype of all religions, is still widespread in Vietnam today. Everything is alive and possessed of a soul. Every tree, every bush, every stone is inhabited by a spirit. Good or evil, benevolent or not, brash, coarse or bashful, the spirits are active in Nature and in all spheres of human activity. Every house has its own spirit, with its own altar. The goodwill of the house spirits can be gained by people's behaviour, and naturally also by appropriate offerings. On the other hand, if people are no longer happy with their house spirit, they can dismiss it and look for a better one. It can be as simple as that.

All Vietnamese are united by the practice of ancestor worship, no matter what religion they profess. It is the basis of the state and of the family. The ancestors still live in and with their families for generations, participating in family life, and are kept informed of everything. They are also believed to give comfort and advice in difficult situations. So no individual is ever alone, but is a link in an unending chain of ancestors and descendants. The altar to the ancestors stands in the largest room in the house, and is well supplied with tea, fruit and other offerings, and incense is burned; these are the prerequisites for communing with the ancestors. When a death occurs, the entire family assembles. The eldest son, who

is responsible for the continuance of the family, supervises the careful carrying out of the ritual, so that the soul of the recently deceased does not have to wander about homeless and with no contacts. Thus not only the family, but the entire nation is linked together. This cohesion may well explain how the Vietnamese have managed to hold their own against enemies who appear unbeatable: the Chinese, the French, the Japanese, and the Americans. In this context, Ho Chi Minh too is a father, a venerable ancestor of the nation.

The Vietnamese adopted Confucianism in the first century BC, during the period of Chinese rule in the north of the country. The name of the founder of this religion was *Kong Quiu*[8] – in Vietnamese *Khong Tu* – the Jesuits transformed it into the Latinate Confucius. Confucius (511-479 BC) was first of all a teacher, then a Mandarin, and was at one point even Justice Minister. His teaching is not a religion promising happiness, but a set of practical instructions for daily life.

33. Street merchant

34. Street merchant

35. Saleswoman

36. Barber working
   from the street

It liberated ancestor worship from magical practices and is based on the belief that a society can only flourish when it has a firm moral basis. Confucius was therefore a moralist who regarded the decline in morals as the cause of the decline of the kingdom. His teaching started from the conviction that only education and achievement should define the path of each individual in a patriarchal society. A promising new beginning could therefore only be successful in conjunction with the Five Virtues: loyalty, honesty, wisdom, right conduct and sincerity. But Confucianism was strictly conservative and would not accept the historical process of change; it became rigid and thus paved the way for the colonial period.

As is so often the case, Confucius found no recognition during his lifetime, but only about 300 years later, when the then rulers dedicated a temple to him and made offerings. They established academies in which the qualifications for the posts to be filled had to be gained by the relevant examinations. In Confucianism, everything is based on maintenance of hierarchies and precise observation of rituals, within the family as well as within the state. The various colonial powers did nothing to alter this as it worked to their advantage. In spite of the limited ability of Confucianism to adapt to change, the Vietnamese still rely on it today, since it reveals a similar inner order to that of the Vietnamese communists, who likewise maintain a strict hierarchy. This is perhaps not surprising when it is remembered that many of the early Vietnamese Communists were educated as Confucian scholars. This firmly rooted structure may also explain why the Communist parties of China and Vietnam have not yet disintegrated.

More or less contemporary with Confucius were Buddha[9] (around 560-480 BC - the available dates are contradictory) in India, and Zarathustra[10] (born around 630BC-date of death unknown) in Persia. Legends narrate that

37. Women's hair salon
38. Beverage stand

Siddhartha, a member of the Gotama family, was born in 623 BC and that he was the son of the ruler of Sakya (a kingdom on the border of Nepal) and his wife Maya. The sources are agreed that he died at the age of 80 in Kusinara in what is now Uttar Pradesh, India. Buddha left no writings; his teachings were spread by his followers. For about 45 years he travelled around, teaching people of all social classes. The beginnings of Buddhism date back to the mid-5th century BC. Subsequently many schools developed, offering different interpretations, and the teachings were more widely disseminated. By the third century BC Buddhism was already being taught and practiced outside its country of origin. It arrived in Vietnam in the first or second century AD, and has been the predominant religion since the 10th century. From time to time it has even been declared the state religion because of the great influence wielded at the royal court by Buddhist monks. Today Buddhism is still the most widely practiced religion in Vietnam.

Zarathustra was the founder of a religion in early Persia. The hymns are only partly preserved in the "Hymns (*Gathas*) of the Awesta", a manuscript which has come down to us in an ancient Iranian language and which, together with a commentary, forms the Holy Scriptures of Zoroastrianism. According to this teaching, the universe is divided into two opposing camps. The Good is allocated to the God Ahura Mazda, the Evil to the God Angra Manju. Ahura Mazda created the original, virtuous humanity and the first animal. Zarathustra's teaching was almost completely superseded by the rise of Islam. In Iran there are now only about 30,000 believers, mainly elderly, who are often from wealthy families.

Attempts at Christian proselytising, led by Portuguese and Italian Dominicans and Jesuits, later followed by their French and British colleagues, began in 1615 in Hoi An, but without leading to any great, or long-lasting, success. Only the French missionary Alexandre de Rhodes[11] (1591-1660), who expanded the Latin alphabet by using extra symbols, is reputed to have converted some of the nobility to Catholicism, thanks to his knowledge of Vietnamese. However under French colonial rule the number of Catholics increased significantly, especially in the North; but after partition these Catholics fled to the non-Communist South, in fear of their lives. During the reign of the Catholic dictator Diem, who employed many Catholics in leading government posts, there were about two million Catholics in South Vietnam.

There is another religious movement which began, according to its founder "Mad Monk" Huynh Phu So[12] (1920-1947), on "the 18th day of the 5th moon-month" (4th July) in 1939. This is the sect of Hoa Hao, which describes itself as reformed Buddhism and aims to provide guidance for everyday life. It is almost exclusively confined to South Vietnam and is said to have about five million followers, claiming to be the third largest religious community in Vietnam "with a phenomenal word-wide growth rate". The religious headquarters are located in the Hoa Hao temple, which was previously a large private estate, where believers meet annually to hold their ceremonies.

In 1919, the spirit Cao Dai is alleged to have appeared to Ngo Van Chieu, an employee of the French colonial administration, in the form of an eye enclosed

in the upper section of a triangle. Within this context "Cao" signifies "high", and "Dai" "house" or "palace", indicating the highest level at which God rules. This spirit is also alleged to have appeared to other people, young French and Vietnamese alike, at the end of 1925. In 1926, or possibly 1927[13], Ngo Van Chieu founded the syncretic Cao-Dai sect. He assumed the title "Pope" to lead the sect which supported a reformed Buddhism uniting all Vietnamese philosophies. The sect was also open to women, and this was the reason it spread so rapidly. As regards content, it preaches the immortality of the soul and seeks to unite all previous religious teachings within itself. It created previous unknown social welfare institutions. It later transformed itself into a political organisation, uniting with the Japanese to oppose the colonial regime, and even managed to equip a 25,000 strong private standing army under the leadership of the "Pope". This army later formed an alliance with the Viet Minh.

The Divine Eye, the symbol of this sect, is depicted on the globe in the cathedral at its headquarters (Holy See) in Tay Ninh, about 100 km northwest of Saigon. At the altar the devotees worship God, symbolised by the Eye, also Buddha, Lao Tse as the apostle of Taoism, Jesus, Confucius, the French writer Victor Hugo[14],

41. Along the promenade

and Trang Trinh; Sun-Yat-Sen [15], the Chinese leader, is also worshipped as a great saint. Today this sect is believed to have about one and a half million members, confined to largely South Vietnam (although it also has some followers in the USA). Caodaism is thus the fourth largest religious grouping in Vietnam.

However varied the religious denominations may be, they all co-exist in peace, after a difficult and restrictive time immediately following re-unification. The reason for this is that the common basis of all Vietnamese religion was, and remains, ancestor worship. This is certainly the reason why a central position is reserved for Ho Chi Minh in many temples and pagodas.

Arts and Crafts

Three areas of Vietnamese art are particularly interesting: ceramics, painting and lacquer-work. The oldest examples of ceramics date from the later Neolithic period and were found in the North, close to Hoa Binh. Later finds include vases decorated with geometric patterns, lamps and urns. During the

medieval period Vietnamese pottery, with different colourings according to the dynasty, was renowned and in great demand as far afield as China and Japan. Apart from today's industrial mass production, which is still from time to time exported to former fellow Communist countries, there are still some schools were the old techniques of craft production are taught, especially for elegant teapots and hand-painted elephants, which are used as small tables with matching stools.

Concerning painting, for the first one and a half millennia there is nothing from Vietnam comparable to that of China and Japan, where painters were members of the imperial household and produced splendid watercolours and pen-and-ink drawings. The influence of the French Impressionists was noticeable during the colonial period. Many works by Vietnamese painters show considerable empathy with Nature; they use similar, repeated motifs that are frequently only indicated in outline. The art of wood-block printing originating in China, was known in Vietnam from the 11th century in the form of simple black and white designs, while coloured prints were available form the 15th century onwards.

42. Board game
on the promenade

Today one frequently sees modified New Year pictures displaying rustic motifs – a cockerel or chrysanthemum as a symbol of luck, a pig as a symbol of prosperity – in strong, bright colours.

Lacquer-work, however, is probably the best known of all the Vietnamese arts and crafts, and the most popular with the comparatively few tourists. The lacquer-work, with its filigree motifs, is produced both for ornament and for utilitarian purposes. The resin for the varnish is obtained from the sumac tree, the cay son, which is cultivated primarily in the Mekong Delta but is also found in the highlands. The whitish resin is gradually applied to the base in many layers. The base has to be smoothed and polished and overlaid with a bonding material if any unevenness remains, before it can be prepared with a fixative. Only then can the first of at least twelve layers of varnish – each of which has to be left to dry for at least a week – be applied. Thus even a simple piece of lacquer-work can take at least three months to complete. In the era of mass production, the amount of time needed to produce a piece of lacquer-work of 100 layers – 200 layers for particularly exquisite pieces – can scarcely be imagined. It is quite understandable that collectors are prepared to pay high prices for these precious objects. The ground colour of the varnish is obtained by mixing the powdered

43. On the Saigon River

wings of cockroaches with cinnabar to obtain a red or dark-red colouring, which is used primarily to cover statues. In order to obtain brighter colours, the powder is mixed with eggshells, either duck, goose or hen depending on the shade required. The marquetry designs in mother-of-pearl (previously derived from real pearl oyster and now mainly artificially produced) are also given a protective coating of lacquer.

There are other branches of art and craft, especially sculpture, bamboo furniture and bamboo musical instruments, which are often made by family businesses, and also traditional hand-embroidery, but they all play a minor role in comparison to ceramics and lacquer-work.

Economy

There are few recent statistics about the economic development of the country. The following estimates, which refer to the mid-1990s, should not blind us to one thing: Vietnam is still a poor country, suffering from the loss of financial support from the former Soviet Union, the aftermath of the long wars, and soaring population growth. It is not yet able to cope with cut-throat international

44. On the Saigon River

Following pages:
45. On the Saigon River

MIẾU CÂY DƯƠNG

KHU PHỐ I PHƯỜNG AN KHÁNH QUẬN 2

competition, especially in heavy industries such as coal, steel, mechanical engineering, paper and cement. In recent years, economic growth reached 9%, although this is based on the unusually low start point, resulting from the severe devastation of the war years. Foreign investment amounts to about two billion US dollars per annum – it is gradually increasing as confidence grows in the capabilities, productivity and reliability of the population. The necessary structural reforms for the revival of the entire economy are steadily being implemented, and previously state-owned firms are being privatised. About 30% of Vietnam's GNP comes from the industrial and agricultural sectors (rice, tea, coffee, potatoes, soya beans), and the service sector accounts for about 40%. In 2001 the export of industrial products earned US$ 3.8 billion, while crude oil earned US$ 3.1 billion. In 2000, a worker's yearly income amounted to roughly US$ 1,300, and that of an engineer to US$ 2,300. There was 25% unemployment.

46. Monument dedicated to Tran Hung Dao

47. A Post Office illustrating French influence in architecture

CHOLON – *formerly Chinatown*

At the turn of the 17th and 18th centuries, the Chinese who had migrated from southern China founded what is now the district of Cholon (meaning "large market") about 5 km from the centre, north of the Ben-Nghe canal. The Chinese had played an important role in Vietnamese history, especially in the North, as conquerors and as a military occupying power, as well as the importers of culture and founders of religions. They fled to South Vietnam during the Ming dynasty [17] and brought with them not only culture and religion, but also hitherto unknown technologies. They soon became an important element in the economy – this is still evident today –and gradually gained pre-eminence in commerce. Their heyday was the French colonial period, and they also flourished under the Americans until 1975. Many Chinese, fearing reprisals, left the city at the same time as the Americans, and most emigrated to the USA. Today there are about one million inhabitants of Cholon; they are assumed to be 50% Chinese and 50% Vietnamese, running shops and family businesses. Districts 1 (Town Centre) and 5 (Cholon) are linked by bus routes which follow several wide roads. Thus Line 1 goes from the well-known Ben-Thanh market, via Tran Hung Do, to the bus station Binh Tay.

The Town Centre

Anyone who is familiar with Bangkok (Thailand) from the 1990s will recognise one similarity with Saigon: the incredible amount of motorbikes. Their number has exploded recently, from 50,000 a few years ago to over one million today, and this is undoubtedly seen as a symbol of the economic upturn. The politics of commercial openness, which is known here as "*doi moi*", is similar to the *perestroika* of Gorbachev's Russia [18]. What was a sleepy provincial backwater at the beginning of the 1990s has suddenly become an extremely dynamic and lively city – accompanied, however, by the negative side-effects of infernal traffic noise, unceasing horn blasts, traffic jams and air pollution.

Traffic

Saigon is not a place for blind people without guides. There are mopeds, bicycles and scooters in motion everywhere, and also often parked at right-angles to one another; an ideal training ground for hurdlers who, however, would also need to watch out for unexpected obstacles. All this has led to a ban on the import of second-hand motorbikes, and only about 8,000 new ones per annum are allowed into the country. These have to share the streets with tricycles, ordinary bicycles – which are heavily laden and used to transport all sorts of objects – and relatively few cars. In spite of extensions on many routes, the roads are still inadequate for the volume of traffic. Are you looking for the road traffic equivalent to a suburb of hell? Then visit Saigon. People drive on the right. Usually. In fact it is more a question of random driving, only occasionally controlled by traffic lights. Without resort to the law of the jungle, everyone moves as fast and as

52. Interior of Notre Dame cathedral

53. Orchid

54. Fresh-water bird in a zoo

55. An elephant in a zoo

skilfully as they can, and they all use the middle of the road, as the kerbs are not particularly navigable and are sometimes occupied by hot food stalls and other street vendors. In practice the Vietnamese do not always obey the traffic laws — although these certainly do exist — but drive in such a way that oncoming traffic in one's own lane is a possibility that has to be reckoned with. If there is still not enough room, people drive on the pavement. Pedestrians, already a minority, although not yet declared a protected species, can only resort to forward flight while crossing the road; he who hesitates is lost. There is only one rule for pedestrians — just keep going, because every driver will overtake you. This can be the only reason why among all this chaos the sound of squealing tyres is never heard and there are hardly any accidents; everyone remains calm and defuses complicated situations with a smile.

None of this prevents the young Saigonese from driving around for hours on their motorbikes, especially in the evenings and at weekends, alone, in pairs or in groups, dressed in their best, following the motto — see and be seen. Older Saigonese, used to the peacefulness of the earlier years, can only watch this change with astonishment as they go for their evening strolls — if they still do. Even an ordinary Saturday evening is worth seeing from this point of view. But what happens on New Year's Eve must be unique in the world; everything with wheels goes on an unstoppable procession through the town, lasting for hours. The vehicles are in rows of five or six, and each accommodates up to five people (sometimes a conveyance can be occupied by three generations of the same family). The whole procession is shrouded in a huge cloud of exhaust fumes. It is pure pleasure in driving, since no one stands on the pavement to watch. Everyone circulates, everyone drives — until midnight. Then the big firework display begins, and the exhaust fumes slowly rise into the dark night sky, gradually mingling with the fireworks.

Ky Khoi Nghia is the Conference Hall — today the Palace of Unity or Palace of Re-unification. This was previously the residence and government headquarters of the President of South Vietnam.

Small Businesses

In the main streets and the wide boulevards there are of course perfectly normal shops in which many items can be purchased. But in the little side streets, merchandise is often quite simply displayed on a cloth on the pavement. This is not only the case in front of the big covered markets, inside which everything is sold from ordinary market stalls, but in front of which a cheese seller might display her home-made cheese on crates, or a melon seller might be awaiting customers in front of piles of green and yellow melons. Meat-vendors sit on little plastic stools, with fillets, giblets, cutlets and bones displayed before them, an attraction to customers and flies alike.

In another street a young shoe-seller, leaning casually against the wall, will have piled up his stock of sports shoes and trainers in multiple rows, while elsewhere oil-changes for motorbikes can be effected on the pavement, as can the repair of burst tyres or the replacement of inner tubes. A barber will sit his cus-

57. Historical museum

58. Dragon on the museum roof

tomers down in front of a small mirror, with a view of the garden wall, and cut their hair while chatting casually; but of course the ladies will sit next to one another in the salon.

A Walk Along the Riverside

The riverbank really only comes to life in the evening. In the morning it is only enlivened by a few exercise fanatics and by the crowds of people who have crossed by ferry from the other bank with their cycles, mopeds and motorbikes. In the evening the brightly-lit restaurant boats wait for customers, and offer a free evening concert of loud music, which is also enjoyed by courting couples who have nowhere else to go. There are also several hot food stalls and a berth for the ferries coming from the opposite bank. Some people fall asleep on the promenade, or children take a nap when they are tired of playing. At Me Linh Square, the northern end of the promenade terminates in a park with splendid bonsai trees- at the southern end it terminates in a discotheque. A little further on, you can cross the Ben-Nghe Canal to the former Dragon House, now the Ho Chi Minh Museum, which has a strong military guard. It is floodlit at night and looks really beautiful.

The Opera House

The Opera House is built to a Parisian model. It was completed in 1899 and opened with great ceremony. There is room for 800 visitors, and during the

Cathedral and leading diagonally to it, is about 40 m wide. It was originally called Boulevard Norodom and was designed by the colonial administration for military parades. The Zoological Garden with its sculptured figures is also here, but this is not particularly worth seeing. On the left of the entrance to the garden is the Historical Museum (formerly the National Museum) built in 1929. This houses interesting collections from the pre-historic and Neolithic periods, numerous artefacts from various Asiatic peoples and Vietnamese dynasties, a collection of pottery and Cham sculpture, and finally a standing bronze Buddha from the 4th or 6th century. In the gardens there is a memorial temple to the Hung Emperors (*Den Tho Hung Vuong*). The area is bordered on the north side by the Thi Nghe canal, which flows into the Song Sai Gon.

The War Museum

Near the Botanical Gardens is the War Museum, easily recognisable by the tank and jet fighter displayed outside, and mainly worth visiting by those who are interested in obsolete American, Chinese and Russian weapons.

66. City Hall

The Town Hall

The Town Hall, built between 1901 and 1908, and still sometimes known as "Hotel de Ville", is now the headquarters of the City Council of Saigon, and is therefore only accessible to foreign visitors by special permission. In 1911 Antoine Brebion wrote this about the building:

"The Hotel de Ville is a costly building, cluttered with ledges, stucco heads and false pillars, crowned with a mutilated clock tower following the models of pavilions in a style reminiscent of Vespasian[25] and Rambuteau[26]. Two huge balconies with railings support the main body of the building up to the level of the first floor. The whole construction is an example of bad taste. We shall therefore refrain from mentioning the names of the two architects who spent nearly ten years, from 1900 to 1908, devising the plans for this building."[27]

There is hardly anything to add to this, except that it may be worth mentioning that there is a remarkable statue of a young-looking Ho Chi Minh outside the building.

67. Tower of Town Hall
68. Conference Hall

The Conference Hall (Palace of Re-Unification)

The present-day Conference Hall, located in a large park and accessible via Nam Ky Khoi Nghia, was originally the Palais *Norodom*, built between 1860 and 1873 by the French colonial administration. Building work was halted during the Franco-Prussian War of 1870-71, which explains the comparatively lengthy construction period.

During the period when the South Vietnamese government was in power, the building was attacked twice – in 1962 and 1975 – by pilots who evidently no longer had faith in the President's loyalty to his people and therefore attacked the building with their helicopters. (One of these helicopters is exhibited on the roof of the building, with an indication of the destination of the bombs). The Presidential residence and government headquarters sustained substantial damage on both occasions. (The first time, the President was Diem; the second time, the equally infamous Nguyen Van Thieu [28]). Neither President, however, seems to have been particularly affected by the attacks, and both stole away through the well-maintained tunnel network under the building. The network contains briefing rooms and a central command post. The ruins were removed and new premises were erected covering an area of about 2,000 square metres. The new building is six storeys high, but two of these are underground. There is still a landing pad for helicopters on the roof – after all, one never knows when it may come

69. Conference Hall

70. Conference Hall

71. Ho Chi Minh
    museum at night
72. Ho Chi Minh museum

in useful. The Hall can be visited today on payment of an entrance fee. It is also known as the Palace of Re-Unification (*Dinh Thong Nhat*) and is used primarily as a venue for congresses and exhibitions.

Museum of War Crimes

To the northeast of the Conference Hall, at Vo Van Tan, is the Museum of War Crimes, aptly housed in the previous headquarters of the American Secret Service, and containing a large quantity of American weapons, vehicles and aeroplanes. To complete the exhibition, the inner courtyard displays one of the most successful inventions of the human mind – and in which sphere have people shown themselves more inventive than in the taking of life? – the *guillotine*[29], which was still in use in the 1960s.

The population was always directly exposed to the effects of weapons of war. The indirect results of the "defoliation action", as well as the "successful" use of poison gases such as Agent Orange[30] only became apparent much later. Agent Orange, a herbicide containing Dioxin, was sprayed during the "American War", together with other herbicides and an insecticide – (all with code names such as Agent Blue and Agent White) – in order to destroy fields and woods. Dioxins are highly toxic and carcinogenic. There are two glass cabinets exhibiting deformed foetuses. The genetic make-up of their mothers had been severely damaged by the poison gases. There is a souvenir shop at the entrance to the museum which offers a special tourist attraction in the form of plastic toy weapons to take home for the children.

Other Markets

A little to the northwest of the Ben Thanh market, on the street Pham Viet Chanh, there is another market, specialising in alternative medicine – this includes dried or pickled snakes. There is a fish-market in the southwest of the city, at Nguyen Thai Hoc near the Ben-Nghe canal. The market of Cho Quan is also on this canal, although it is nearer to Cholon. The huge, fascinating market of Cholon, still surrounded by a few open-air markets, is next to the western terminus of Bus Route 1. This dates from 1928, and it may not be possible to visit it for very much longer as it may be scheduled for demolition. This is one of the most colourful, exciting, lively bazaars in Saigon, covering an area of more than 10,000 square meters and probably offering the greatest range of goods in the whole of Vietnam.

Temples and Pagodas

The term "pagoda" is of Indo-Malay origin. It refers to the tower-like temple buildings of wood, stone or iron, often with circular or polygonal ground plans, that are found throughout South-East Asia. The buildings are often adorned with representations of animals – for instance, a turtle as the sign of long life, a

phoenix as a symbol of peace and prosperity, or a dragon, a symbol of the Emperor and the attribute of immortality. There are about 180 temples and pagodas in Saigon. The oldest is the Chinese pagoda Giac Lam, located away from the centre in the northwestern district 10. It is worth seeing, as it has remained unaltered since it was built in the 18th century. For structural reasons it was constructed as a low wooden building in a deep foundation pit. The lacquered icons of ancestors attract attention in the foyer. The main building is divided into three sections and surrounded by a garden. There is a dining room, a common room, and a temple where the eye is immediately drawn to the 118 gilded statues on the altar. The altar carvings depict the Nine Dragons — nine branches of the Mekong. There are further splendid carvings on the sidewalls, depicting the Judges of Hell.

78. Giac Lam pagoda

79. Monk in the inner
    courtyard of the
    Giac Lam pagoda

Following pages

80. Altar in the Temple of the
    Jade Emperors

There is another remarkable temple in the District of Bin Than, north of the city centre. It is in the centre of what was previously Gia Dinh (the name of the nearby Post Office is a reminder of this) on a site covering about 10,000 square metres, and is dedicated to one of the greatest figures of Vietnamese history, Le Van Duyet (1763-1832).

Le Van Duyet, whose portrait adorns the altar, was a general. He successfully opposed a rebellion, was equally successful as an administrative and economic expert, and united the districts of Saigon and Cholon.

81. Altar in the Temple of the Jade Emperors
82. Temple of the Jade Emperors

District 1

In a central location in Troung Dinh, close to the Ben Thanh market, there is a temple dedicated to the Goddess Mari Amman. There are two Hindu temples in the vicinity of Le Loi Street – this one to the north, the other to the south – whose congregations include Tamils, Chinese and many Vietnamese.

This one is the more striking as it contains countless depictions of gods, people and animals. There are other, larger temples in District 1, north and west of the centre. For instance, west of the Botanical Gardens and next to the Da Kao market, is the temple of the Jade Emperor, built in 1909. Externally it looks nothing out of the ordinary, but the interior is

83. Temple of the Jade Emperors
84. Thien Hau Temple

85. Insense from the Temple /
    Greetings vanish into the air
86. Insense from the Temple /
    Greetings vanish into the air

very striking. Here one can see the splendid green figure of the Jade Emperor, the chief God of the Taoists, with his fierce guardians. An altar is in front of the figure, and six further statues behind it, guardians and gods of the North and South Pole Stars.

The King of Hell with three gods can be seen behind the altar to the right, and in the room beyond there are carvings of twelve small female figures, images of the Chinese calendar. The temple of Tran Hung Do is located about 500 m further on, in Duong Vo Thi Sau. Near the Russian Embassy, between Nguyen Huyen Than, there is a relatively new temple, Xa Loi, erected in 1956.

This played a role in recent history as a centre of resistance against Diem's regime, and 400 monks and nuns were imprisoned here on the orders of Diem's brother. Finally, there is another temple, Ky Vien, near the Festival Hotel between Caa Thang and Ban Co, and close to it is a very lively market.

Cholon

In the centre of Cholon there are six pagodas in a relatively small area, only a few hundred metres apart. The first three noteworthy temples are close to the bus terminus Binh Tay: Tam San Hoi Quan, close to it Thien Hau and finally, An Hoi Quan. The most important of these is undoubtedly Thien Hau, which was built in 1847 and dedicated to Buddha and his

female counterpart, the Goddess of the Sea and Protectress of Sailors. The entry is guarded by dragons, the symbols of power and fortune. In the inner courtyard there are huge ancient bronze vessels with incense burners.

The bronze bell dates from 1830 and rings whenever a large donation is made. Visitors write their wishes for better health or better business on amulets. There is a strong scent of incense in the air. There are shelves containing brightly coloured ceramic figures of characters from Chinese mythology.

The temple of An Hoi Quan, dedicated to the Goddess of Charity, is close by. This was built at the beginning of the 19th century and has some connections with Quan Cong, a third century Chinese general of the Three Kingdoms, who carries a stick in his hand and thus functions as a watchman. In an side room he is shown together with the Goddess Quan An, who is clad entirely in white. A beautiful carved boat hangs just by the entrance.

Visitors are greeted by an larger-than-life statue of the Emperor's horse. There is a third temple in this area, which almost seems to be the religious quarter; this is the Pagoda Tam Son Hoi Quan, also built in the 19th century. Here the goddess of fertility is worshipped, and thus the temple is primarily visited by women. Further along this relatively narrow street is the Ha Chuong pagoda.

87. Dragon festival at the Thien Hau Temple
88. Dragon festival at the Thien Hau Temple

Cu Chi

About a day's journey northwest of Saigon is the Cu Chi Tunnel complex, which gives a vivid impression of the desperate fighting of the Vietnamese during the "American War".

The area above ground is covered with bomb craters and rusty out-of-commission tanks. Young saplings are gradually growing up through the craters. It was an area in which crafty, invisible traps caused incredible sufferings to those who sprung them, and increased the soldiers' feelings of insecurity.

There was an underground area, invisible through the foliage, which was as much as three stories deep (to a depth of up to 12 m), containing kitchens, conference and strategic rooms, and sanitary facilities. Even the Vietnamese had to stoop in the communicating tunnels, which covered an area of about 200 km and led as far as Saigon. This network of tunnels symbolised the gate of hell to many American soldiers. It was never captured and could not be destroyed, in spite of the use of tracker dogs, flame-throwers, bombs, state-of-the-art equipment and courageous soldiers. Here is a place where Vietnamese history was written, and it also explains why the Americans could not win this war.

89. Dragon festival at the Thien Hau Temple
90. Dragon festival at the Thien Hau Temple
91. Dragon festival at the Thien Hau Temple

Conclusion

What does Saigon have to offer a visitor today? It is a young town, which only celebrated its 300th anniversary in 1998, with a short but exciting history; lively, vibrant, and only quiet in the very early mornings. The citizens are friendly people. There is a huge density of population, and the traffic is chaotic and cacophonous, so that even crossing the road is an adventure. It was first of all built in the 19th century following the principles of Parisian town planners, with wide boulevards and colonial style buildings that are still worth seeing. During the decades of American presence in the 20th century, the city was expanded by American architects. Embedded in Chinese and Vietnamese culture with oases of rest, this town is a conglomeration of its history. Its future has only just begun, with a period of rapid growth and the gradual liberalisation of trade and industry in a Communist State.

92. Entrance to the
    Cu Chi tunnels

93. Decorations for the New Year

94. balloons for the New Year

History

After the 3ʳᵈ millenium BC	Invasion of present-day north Vietnam by Austronesians and Malay peoples
From 7ᵗʰ to 4ᵗʰ century BC	Invasion of the Viets from Southern China
From 111 BC to 939 AC	Occupation and domination of Northern Vietnam by China
From 7ᵗʰ to 15ᵗʰ century	The Cham Empire in Central Vietnam
From 1009 to 1225	Reign of the Ly dynasty, Hanoi is founded
From 1225 to 1400	Reign of the Tran dynasty
From 1428 to 1776	Height of power and victorians against the Cham
From 16ᵗʰ to 17ᵗʰ century	Christian missions and trade with the Europeans
From 1883 to 1939	French colony of Indo-China
From 1940 to 1945	Occupation of Vietnam by Japan. Resistance against Japan
From 1946 to 1954	Restoration of French domination. Resistance against France
From 1954 to 1975	Division of Vietnam between the Democratic Republic of Vietnam (Northern Vietnam) and the Republic of Vietnam (Southern Vietnam)
From 1964 to 1975	The Vietnam War (the "American War")
1975	Reunification of North and South Vietnam under the name Socialist Republic of Vietnam
1979	Conflict with China, exodus of the *boat people*
1991	The 7ᵗʰ Congress of the Communist Party of Vietnam decides on a free-market economy

Bibliography

W.-E. Bühler/H. Kothmann: Vietnam, Reise Know-How-Verlag P. Rump, Bielefeld/Brackwede, 1995.
Th. Barkemeier: Vietnam, DuMont Verlag, Cologne, 2nd edition 2000.
Annaliese Wulf: Vietnam, Pagoden und Tempel, DuMont Verlag, Cologne, 1991.
John R. Jones: Vietnam-Handbuch, C. Stein Verlag, Kiel, 1990.
Hans Illner: Reiseland Vietnam, edition Aragon, 1989.
Polyglott APA-Guide: Vietnam, Langenscheidt KG, Berlin/Munich, 2000.
Saigon Times: No. 08 and 09 of the 16th February 2002.

Notes

1. Alexander VI, born 1 January 1431 or 1432 in Jativa near Valencia, died 18 August 1503 in Rome, most likely from malaria. Source of illustration: Biography of Cethegus.
2. Source: *Vietnam*, W.-E. Bühler and H. Kothmann.
3. Source: ibidem.
4. Born 19 Mai 1890 in Hoang Tru, died 2 September 1969 in Hanoi.
5. Born 21 February 1879 in Gori, died 5 March 1953 in Moscow, Soviet dictator.
6. Born 26 December 1893 in Schao Schan (Hunan Province), died 9 September 1976 in Peking, President of the Communist Party of China, President of the Republic.
7. Source: German National Bureau of Statistics, situation as of January 2002.
8. Confucius born 511, died in 479 BC.
9. Buddha born approximately 560 BC died 480 BC.
10. Zarathoustra born approximately 630 BC, date of death unknown, prophet and religious founder in Ancient Persia.
11. Alexander of Rhodes, born 15 March 1591 in Avignon, France, died 5 November 1660 in Isfahan, Iran, French monk, author and missionary.
12. Born in 1920 in Angiang Province, died in 1947.
13. The documentary sources differ appreciably from one another regarding the date of the founding of the sect, which was probably between 18 and 20 November 1927.
14. Victor Hugo, born 26 February 1802, died 22 May 1885, French poet, adversary of Napoleon III and thus exiled to the Island of Guernesey for numerous years.
15. Sun-Yat-Sen, also known as Sun Wen, born on 12 November 1866, died 12 March 1925, was the instigator of the Chinese Revolution in China in 1911. He was also President of the Republic of China.
16. Graham Greene, born 2 October 1904, died 3 April 1991, English novelist.
17. The Ming dynasty governed China from 1368 to 1644.
18. Mikhail Gorbachev born 2 March 1931 in Privolnoje, USSR, Secretary General of the Soviet Communist Party from 1985 to 1991.
19. First Minister set in place by the last Emperor Bao Dai, who astounded this Emperor by declaring himself President. His own security forces removed him from power on 2 November 1963.
20. Revolutionary government from 18 March to 29 May 1871. Crushed by the troops of the National Assembly.
21. Karl Marx, born 5 May 1818, died 14 March 1883, founder of the Socialist doctrine with Friedrich Engels.
22. Friedrich Engels, born 28 November 1820, died 5 August 1895, principal theorist of Marxism.
23. Vladimir Illich Oulianov commonly known as Lenin, born 22 April 1870, died 21 January 1924, Founder of Leninist doctrine and leader of the Russian revolutionary State.
24. Alexander Gustave Eiffel, born in 1832, died in 1923, French engineer, builder of the Eiffel Tower as well as numerous bridges and shopping centers.
25. Titus Flavius Vespasianus, 9-79AD, Roman Emperor, commissioned the construction of the Coliseum.
26. Rambuteau- Claude Philibert Berthelot, born in 1781, died in 1869, Commander under Napoleon I.
27. Extract of: *Saigon und der Suden Vietnams* - Saigon and Southern Vietnam, by W.E Bühler and H. Kothmann, page 153/54.
28. Nguyen Van Thieu, President-elect of Vietnam from 1967 to 1975.
29. From the name of the French Doctor Guillotin, 1738-1814, an instrument used to execute those sentenced to death.
30. Agent Orange, herbicide containing the dioxin often used by the Americans during the Vietnam War. As well as other herbicides and insecticides, all under secret names such as Agent Blue or Agent White, all were sprayed over fields and forests by plane with the intent to destroy.
31. Soldier fighting for the liberty of Vietnam from the 15th century.
32. Admiral Bonard was the first French Governor of Cochinchine.

95. Greeting cards